For Frank Maher, my partner in all things, and for the people of Bali.

Published by Tuttle Publishing, an imprint of Periplus Editions (HK) Ltd., with editorial offices at
364 Innovation Drive, North Clarendon, Vermont 05759 U.S.A. and at 61 Tai Seng Avenue #02-12, Singapore 534167.

Text and illustrations © 2010 Betty Reynolds

All rights reserved. No part of this publication may be reproduced or utilized in any form or by any means, electronic or mechanical, including photocopying, recording, or by any information storage and retrieval system, without prior written permission from the publisher.

Distributed by

North America, Latin America & Europe
Tuttle Publishing
364 Innovation Drive
North Clarendon, VT 05759-9436 U.S.A.
Tel: 1 (802) 773-8930
Fax: 1 (802) 773-6993
info@tuttlepublishing.com
www.tuttlepublishing.com

Asia Pacific
Berkeley Books Pte. Ltd.
61 Tai Seng Avenue #02-12
Singapore 534167
Tel: (65) 6280-1330
Fax: (65) 6280-6290
inquiries@periplus.com.sg
www.periplus.com

Indonesia
PT Java Books Indonesia
Jalan Rawa Gelam IV No. 9
Kawasan Industri Pulogadung
Jakarta Timur 13930, Indonesia
Tel: (62) 021 4682-1088
Fax: (62) 021 461-0206
cs@javabooks.co.id

ISBN 978-0-8048-4043-9

First edition
13 12 11 10   7 6 5 4 3 2 1

Printed in Malaysia

TUTTLE PUBLISHING® is a registered trademark of Charles E. Tuttle Publishing, Inc., a division of Periplus Editions (HK) Ltd.

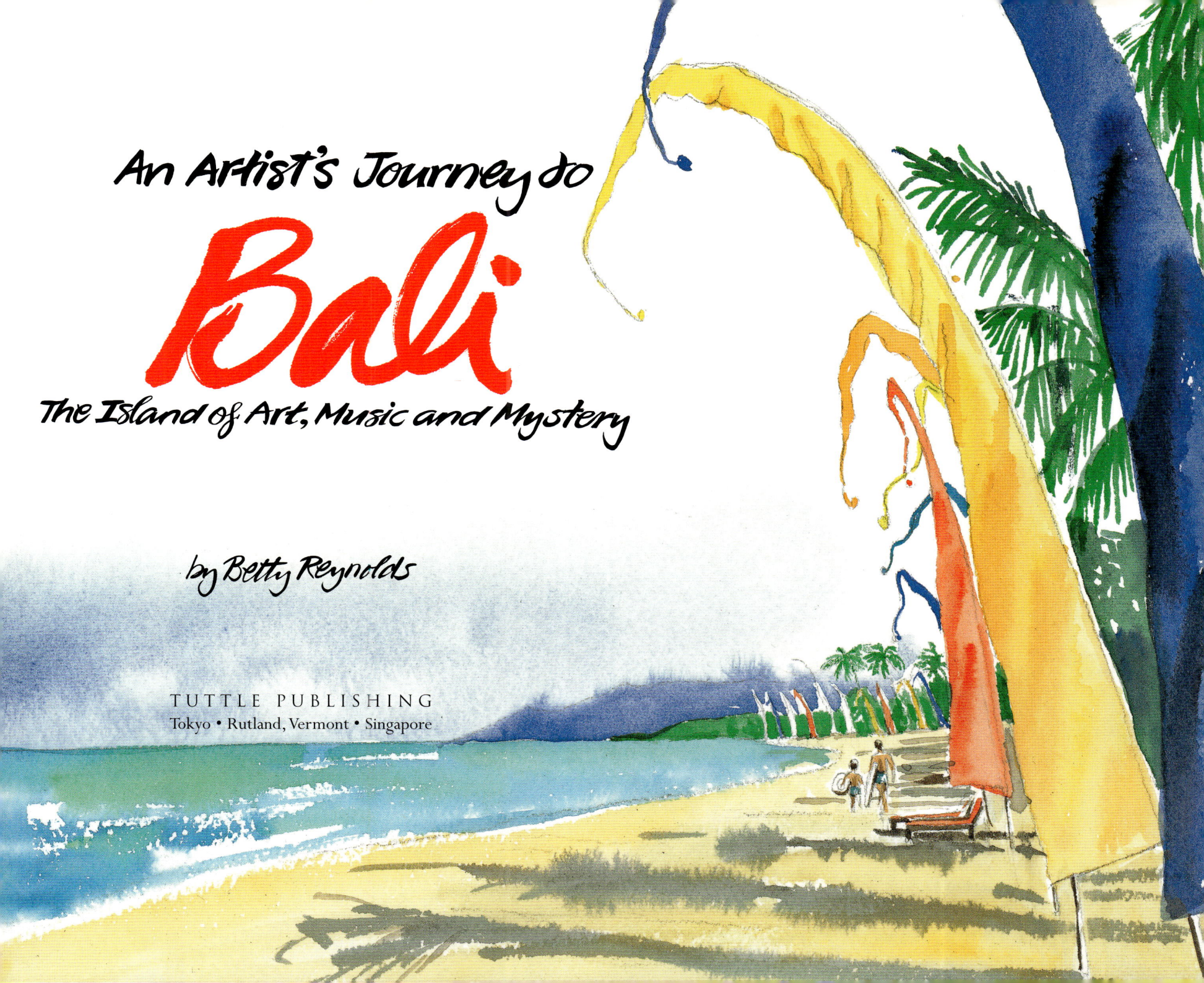

An Artist's Journey to *Bali*

The Island of Art, Music and Mystery

by Betty Reynolds

TUTTLE PUBLISHING
Tokyo • Rutland, Vermont • Singapore

❻ Hiked Gunung Batur and ate an egg cooked in a steam vent

Saw a Balinese baby touch the ground for the first time

Learned how to make a hat made of fruit

Selamat Datang
Welcome!

❼ Watched dance performances in Ubud

Walked many beaches in Southern Bali

W elcome to Bali, the island of beauty and mystery. Over our 20-year association with Asia, my husband and I return here to vacation as often as possible. With each visit, we become more fascinated with the culture and more charmed by the people. We have been fortunate to meet many Balinese people willing to allow us direct exposure to important aspects of their lives and culture. We visited Balinese homes and villages, learned how to pray at temple ceremonies and festivals, and participated in important rituals that mark Balinese passage through the main stages of life. Most importantly, we made friends with a wonderful group of people! This sketchbook records our many experiences. I hope it will be useful, or at least entertaining to those lucky enough to travel here, or for those curious to know what the fuss is all about. Please have a look.

Pulau Dewata
Island of the Gods

why is this volcano considered sacred?

Gunung Agung
This active volcano is thought to be the "navel of the world" and the home of the spirits of Balinese ancestors.

Bali is an island of inviting beaches, imposing mountains and great physical beauty. The topography is dominated by an east-west chain of volcanoes with a multitude of rivers that cut deep ravines as they flow from the highlands to the surrounding sea. The abundance of water and the uncommon fertility of the volcanic soils result in luxurious growth throughout the island. The southern plains are extensively cultivated with rice fields watered by an ancient, complex irrigation system. The spiritual and social lives of the Balinese are strongly influenced by this unique geography. The lofty mountains are believed to be the abode of the Gods; humans live in the middle ground; while the sea below is the domain of evil spirits. This mountain-to-sea axis aligns the layouts of villages, houses and rooms, and orients the Balinese throughout their lives.

What are those decorations in the ricefields?

Banten are offerings to the Gods which accompany every stage of the rice-growing process.

Padi The terraced rice fields of Bali are an artist's paradise with colors changing from green to the yellow-orange hue at harvest time. Rice is the single most important food crop in Bali. Good volcanic soils, plentiful rain and ingenious irrigation networks produce three crops of rice every fourteen months.

What is that procession on the beach?

Sanur and other spectacular beaches attract tourists and serve as a spiritual place for cleansing ceremonies.

Cili is a woven image of the rice goddess Dewi Sri that symbolizes wealth and fertility.

whose face is woven into offerings?

What is the meaning of those ornate poles?

The true magic of Bali lies in her beautiful people and their religion which provides an all-encompassing structure for their lives. The Balinese form of Hinduism evolved over centuries. It is a composite of ancient animistic beliefs and successive waves of Buddhist and Hindu influences from Java. The unique rituals and ceremonies resulting from this mix is the heart of Balinese culture. The Balinese believe their universe is under the influence of competing forces of order and disorder. Their religion is focused on rituals, ceremonies and behavior designed to maintain a balance between these forces. For the average Balinese, dogma and philosophy play little role in religion. A devout Balinese need only make daily offerings and participate fully in village and temple ceremonies.

Poleng are black and white checked fabrics that balance high and low spirits.

Images of gods and demons are evident everywhere in Bali. However, these many gods are all manifestations of the one supreme god, Ida Sanghyang Widhi. One important manifestation is the Trinity [Trisabti] consisting of: Brahma the Creator, Vishnu the Preserver, and Siwa the Destroyer. Their Trinity is embodied in every temple and symbolized by the colors red, white and black in ceremonial cloths and decorations. Also evident are other gods, demons and protective spirits. In keeping with their view of a universe of good and evil, high and low, and *sekala* and *niskala* [the visible and the invisible], the Balinese also believe in black magic, ghosts and evil spirits. Many of their arts were developed to create beautiful and elaborate forms to appease and balance these opposing forces.

why do demons wear checked tablecloths?

Ogoh-Ogoh are fearsome characters on stilts during Nyepi, the Day of Silence.

Penjor are decorative bamboo poles symbolizing fertility that line the streets during Kuningan and Galungan, the two most important festivals in Bali. These offerings are also found in rice fields.

Pura Temples

Who are those frightening creatures guarding the temples?

Monkeys are a constant source of entertainment at the temple complex inside the Monkey Forest Sanctuary.

There are well over 20,000 temples spread throughout Bali. Many of the most important ones are situated dramatically in the mountains and near waterways. Visitors are welcome if they are respectfully dressed in a sarung and sash. Please do not enter if you are menstruating or in mourning.

The inner court contains *pelinggih*, which are shrines and seats for importat deities.
A – The interpreter of the deities
B – Maospahit, the original settlers
C – The volcano Batur
D – The Hindu holy mountain Mahameru
E – The volcano Agung
F – The Sun God
G – The founder of the local village
H & I – The secretaries of the gods who ensure that proper offerings are made
J – A communal seat for the gods

Kala
A symbol of evil thought to ward off demonic influences

Raksasa
Guardians of the inner sanctuary

Kori agung
The gate to the inner area reserved for worship

Candi Bentar
A split gateway

The middle courtyard houses open pavilions for cooking and cock fights.

Hey! What am I looking at?

The outer courtyard has pavilions for gamelan music and visitors.

The Kulkul Tower with a split-log drum.

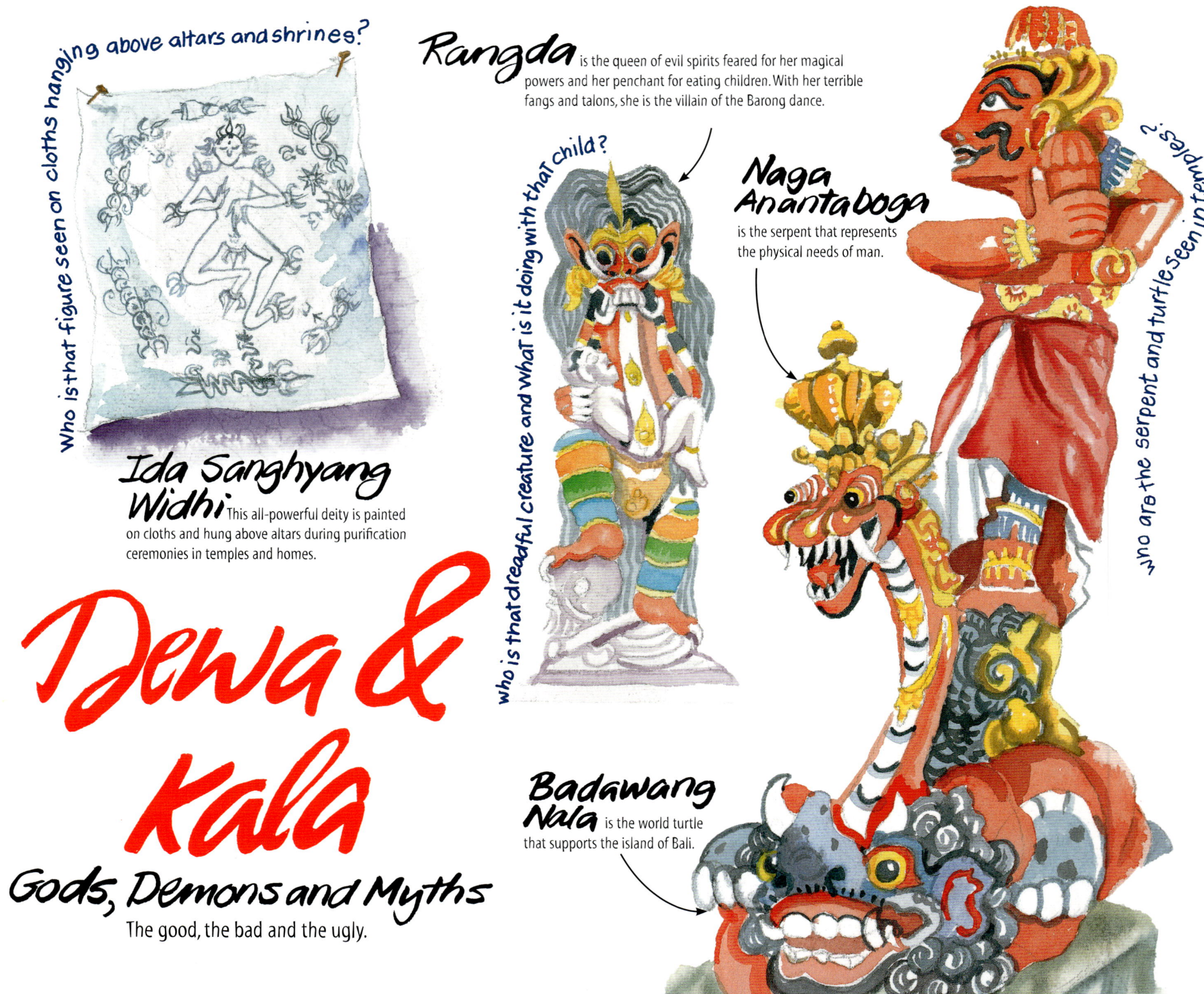

Dewa & Kala
Gods, Demons and Myths
The good, the bad and the ugly.

Who is that figure seen on cloths hanging above altars and shrines?

Ida Sanghyang Widhi This all-powerful deity is painted on cloths and hung above altars during purification ceremonies in temples and homes.

Rangda is the queen of evil spirits feared for her magical powers and her penchant for eating children. With her terrible fangs and talons, she is the villain of the Barong dance.

Who is that dreadful creature and what is it doing with that child?

Naga Anantaboga is the serpent that represents the physical needs of man.

Who are the serpent and turtle seen in temples?

Badawang Nala is the world turtle that supports the island of Bali.

Lingam is a phallic symbol in the Hindu religion. Here, they represent Vishnu, the God of Life and Preservation; Siwa, the God of Destruction and Reincarnation; and Brahma, the God of Creation.

What are these stones? And why are they honored?

Garuda The official mount of the God Siwa in the Ramayana legend is also the symbol of the Indonesian Republic.

Ganesha This Hindu God is the remover of obstacles. He is worshipped before every new undertaking.

Who is that elephant and why is he wielding an axe?

Aren't there any Goddesses?

Saraswati is the Goddess of Wisdom and Learning, worshipped in a ceremony for books every 210 days.

Dewi Sri No stage of rice cultivation would be complete without ceremonies for the Goddess of Rice and Fertility.

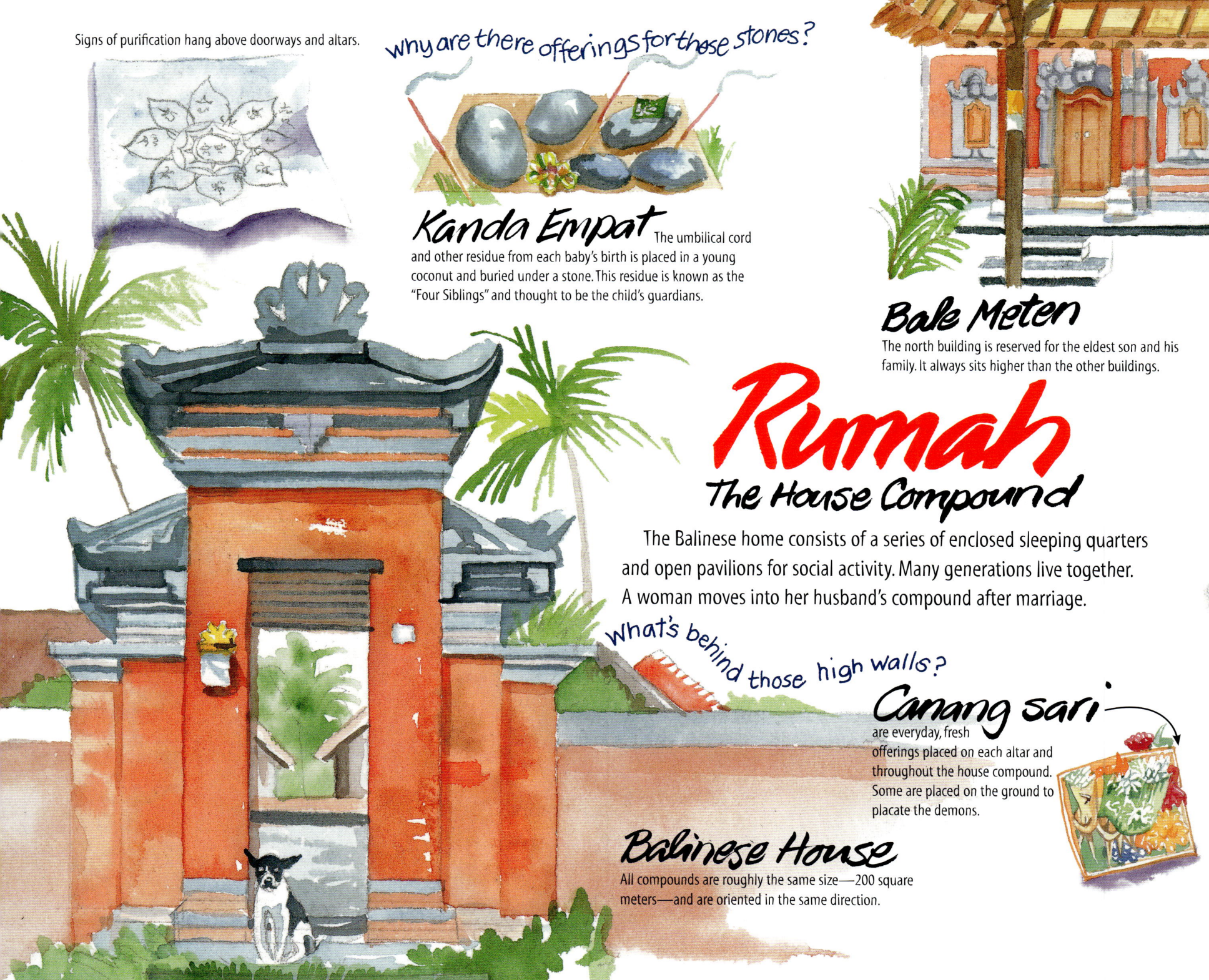

Signs of purification hang above doorways and altars.

Why are there offerings for these stones?

Kanda Empat
The umbilical cord and other residue from each baby's birth is placed in a young coconut and buried under a stone. This residue is known as the "Four Siblings" and thought to be the child's guardians.

Bale Meten
The north building is reserved for the eldest son and his family. It always sits higher than the other buildings.

Rumah
The House Compound

The Balinese home consists of a series of enclosed sleeping quarters and open pavilions for social activity. Many generations live together. A woman moves into her husband's compound after marriage.

What's behind those high walls?

Canang sari
are everyday, fresh offerings placed on each altar and throughout the house compound. Some are placed on the ground to placate the demons.

Balinese House
All compounds are roughly the same size—200 square meters—and are oriented in the same direction.

Sanggah

A house temple is always placed in the northeast corner of the compound. It contains altars and shrines dedicated to the gods, the family's ancestors and the volcanoes Batur and Agung.

What are all those thatch roofs?

Bale Dangin

An open pavilion with a ceremonial bed used for life cycle rituals

Eldest son's sleeping quarters

The family temple

Guest quarters and social pavilion

Entrance — Half wall

The backyard contains animals, useful plants, trees and toilet.

Rice granary

Kitchen

How do you use the toilet?

Straddle and lower yourself (as best as you can) over the toilet. Use a pail of water to cleanse yourself. Please don't put paper in the toilet.

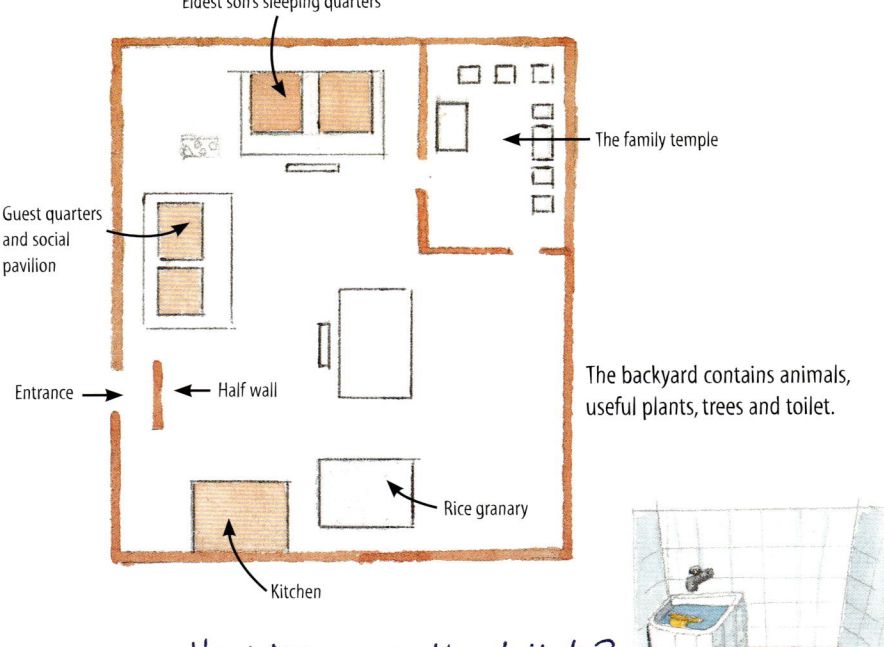

Where do the Balinese shop? I see no supermarkets.

Pasar
Each village has a farmer's market selling fresh produce and other commodities.

Warung
The village shop is both a convenience store and a spot for socializing.

Pura
Each village has at least three temples:
Pura Desa is the temple dedicated to the deities protecting the village. It is the temple most frequently used for ceremonies.
Pura Puseh is for the worship of the founding ancestors of the village.
Pura Dalem, the Temple of the Dead, is for the appeasement of the spirits of the deceased, and is located on the outskirts of the village.

Is it my imagination, or do most villages look alike

Desa
The Balinese Village

The people of Bali live in thousands of villages throughout the island. These villages are laid out in a traditional plan with a mountain-to-sea axis.

Why are there so many temples? What is that drumming I hear?

Kul Kul
are village slit-log drums thtat are beaten to signal births, deaths, fires and other important events.

Pertunjukan Tari Bali
Dance Performances

Balinese dance performances, held on temple grounds and in major hotels are based on old Hindu epic poems, but the stylized movements are said to be purely Balinese. Here are just a few of the more popular dances.

who is that fierce lion?

The Barong
A mythical lion considered to be the guardian of villages, fights off the evil influences of the bad witch/queen Rangda in the energetic and entertaining Barong Dance. It is sometimes called the Kris Trance Dance.

Rangda
and her evil attendants.

chak-ka-chak-ka-chak? What does that mean?

Kecak This dramatic performance features a hypnotic chorus of chants, grunts and screeches simulating the syncopated sounds of a gamelan orchestra. The dance partially depicts an episode from the Ramayana when Rama's wife Sita is kidnapped by the demon-king Rawana. Sita is eventually saved by Hanuman and his monkey army. Once again, good triumphs over evil.

Oh-oh! Will this dance have a happy ending?

Baris is a classic dance celebrating masculinity and military prowess. The Baris can have as many as 60 performers engaged in battle.

The Gamelan Percussion Orchestra

What is that haunting melody?

Terompong and Reyong
Themes and chords are played on a series of gongs suspended in a frame.

Why is a priest on the stage? 
The instruments are purified with holy water before the performance.

Suling
Bamboo flutes lead the melody.

Are the instruments only played by men?
No, in the past ten years women have had their own orchestras.

Balinese dance performances are enhanced by the unique sound of the gamelan. Children are taught to play these traditional instruments by their village banjar. Different types of percussion orchestras accompany cremations and other religious processions.

Kendang
A pair of male/female drums set the rhythm and lead the orchestra.

Gangsa
Metallophones with metal keys of various sizes and pitch play themes and variations.

Cengceng
Tiny cymbals beat out fast rhythms.

Kempli
A pot gong is held in the lap and struck with a padded mallet.

Kempur and Ageng
Suspended bronze gongs provide the accents.

Topeng Masks

Skillfully created masks embody the true personality of characters portrayed in traditional dance performances. Some masks, considered sacred, are kept locked in temples because of their special powers.

Gold and Silver

Gold and silver-smiths make ceremonial as well as functional objects, and jewelry of every variety.

Painting

Balinese paintings are well designed with an amazing number of details. Every leaf in nature, every facet of village life is carefully drawn and skillfully painted with small brushes and pens. You'll probably take home several.

How can one painting contain so much?

Textiles

Beautifully dyed and woven fabrics are deemed essential for ceremonies and rites of passage. The Balinese like rich brocades with gold and silver threads called *songket* and *prada*, and tie-dyed wovens called *endek*. *Batiks* and *ikat* fabrics seem to be tourist favorites. Be sure to buy a *sarung* to wear in the temples.

Manusa Yadnya
Ceremonies and Rites of Passage

Lis are woven offerings that represent the human body and are used to sprinkle holy water during purification rites.

Ceremonies, philosophy, and moral behavior are the three fundamentals of Balinese culture. Besides the ritual daily offerings to the Gods, there are ceremonies performed every five, fifteen and 210 days. The odds are good that you can find a ceremony happening somewhere on the island on any given day.

Life Cycle Rituals

In order to become a better person in this life and to attain Moksa (or Nirvana) in the afterlife, every Balinese is obligated to perform certain rites of passage. These purification ceremonies, held in the family compound, are very elaborate and expensive. Although these events should occur at a certain time in one's life, they are often postponed until the expenses can be shared with other participants.

what is that large cake?

Sarad, a towering offering symbolizing the universe, is made of rice dough cookies covering a bamboo frame.

Does this get eaten?

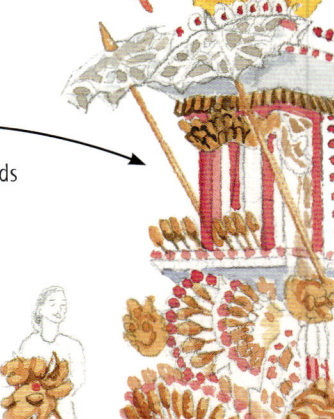

Sate Tegeh

The *sarad*'s counterpart is made with garlands of intestines, sculpted fat and grilled meat skewers, all from a slaughtered pig.

Most temple festivals and rites of passage contain this pair of amazing offerings, which can be ten feet (three meters) tall. Only the gods partake of their essence.

The entrance to the family compound is gaily decorated on the occasion of purification and rites of passage ceremonies.

Is that a Christmas decoration?

Guests arrive bearing humble gifts of bananas or sugar and leave with part of the feast.

Should I bring a gift?

Members of the village banjar contribute to the time-consuming preparations. The slaughtering of pigs; the preparation of a huge feast; and the weaving of intricate, fantastic offerings and decorations become lighter work when shared with a hundred people or more. These spiritual and energy-renewing rituals, attended by extended family, friends and neighbors, are joyous events, which normally last all day. Although the details of the ceremonies vary from village to village, the ones we were privileged to attend all seemed to contain equal parts of religion, socializing and feasting.

During a marriage ceremony, priests recite mantras inviting the Gods and ancestors to enter the family's temple. The bride and groom pray to deified ancestors who will someday be reincarnated into their future offspring.

Guests arrive bearing gifts on their heads.

Bale Dangin
A pavilion in the family compound is decorated and filled with special offerings.

Otonon
Baby's First Birthday

A purification ceremony takes place when a baby is six months old on the Balinese calendar. He or she gets a secret name, a first haircut, and touches ground for the first time.

Kanda Empat
A stone memorializing the baby's four spiritual guardians is covered in offerings.

what is in the clay pot?

Gold jewelry, an egg, and other symbols of development rest inside a clay pot. The baby's hands and feet are dipped in holy water. The proud parents cut off the protective strings that the baby has worn on its wrists and ankles since birth and replace them with gold.

what is the priest making with rice flour?

A priest draws the turtle Empas, which represents the universe, on the rice flour spread on the ground.

The baby's feet are placed on the flour, touching the ground for the first time in his young life.

Jangan
A woven offering invites the spiritual guardians to protect the baby.

Be Guling
Several suckling pigs are enjoyed by the guests and villagers after the gods partake of their essence.

The child is symbolically fed bits of food—sweet, sour, salty and sharp—so that he can taste all that life has to offer.

Why don't I see Balinese babies around?

Babies are considered sacred. They are carefully watched over by extended family members in the compound. Because earth and soil is thought to be the domain of evil spirits and beasts, babies never touch the ground until they are 210 days old.

Attractive young women greet guests at the entrance with a welcome snack of water, a rice packet, and peanuts.

Cili →

The ceremonial bed in the open pavilion is surrounded by woven Cili figures, a symbol of beauty and fertility.

Matatah
The Tooth Filing Ceremony

At the onset of puberty, the four upper front teeth are filed into an even line because they are thought to contain demonic characteristics and evil influences. The filing is also thought to enhance the person's attractiveness. Sometimes this purification and beautification rite is postponed until there are other participants to share the expenses.

Does this mean I can lose my bad habits by filing my teeth?

Sad Ripu

The 'six evils' of man thought to be contained in the six front teeth are:

Kama - lust and desire
Krodha - anger
Lobha - greed
Mada - arrogance and pride
Matsarya - jealousy
Moha - stupidity

Bad look

Good look

Performers reciting ancient poems entertain the guests between purification rites.

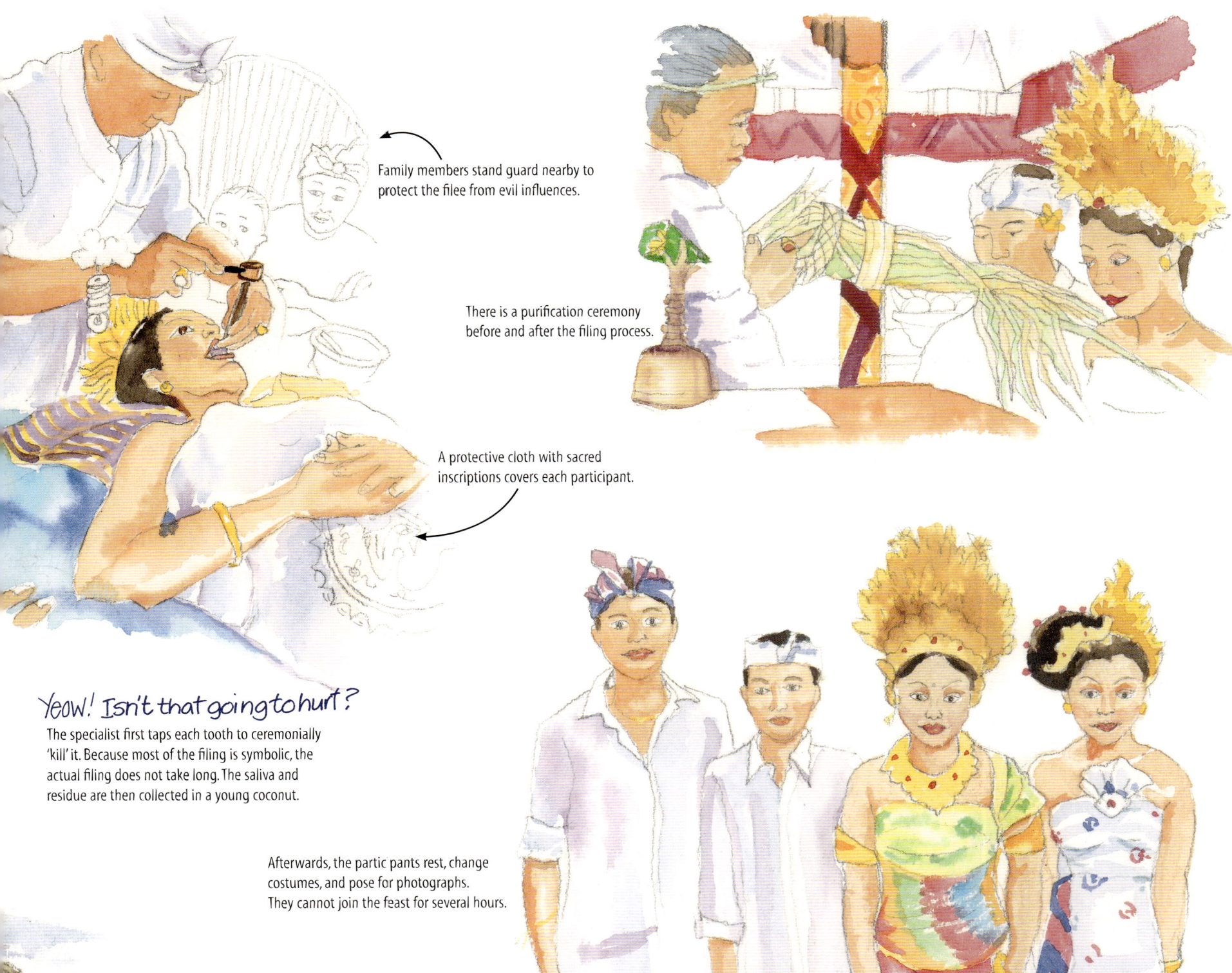

Family members stand guard nearby to protect the filee from evil influences.

There is a purification ceremony before and after the filing process.

A protective cloth with sacred inscriptions covers each participant.

Yeow! Isn't that going to hurt?

The specialist first taps each tooth to ceremonially 'kill' it. Because most of the filing is symbolic, the actual filing does not take long. The saliva and residue are then collected in a young coconut.

Afterwards, the partic pants rest, change costumes, and pose for photographs. They cannot join the feast for several hours.

MabyaKala
Marriage Ceremony

When a young couple decides to marry, the boy visits the girl's home three times for a series of discussions. The boy takes his parents along on the first visit to help present his merits and exchange gifts. On the second visit, the bride and groom's extended families meet to prepare the couple for the responsibilities of marriage. On the third visit, the boy's banjar leader accompanies the groom and his parents to register the groom's intent and set a date for the wedding. This is quite an undertaking, especially if the couples live far apart. Often, a young couple will elope to avoid this lengthy, expensive process.

At the ceremony in the groom's compound, an aunt carries a basket containing the bride's trousseau.

The groom carries a bamboo pole with items grown on his compound at each end, symbolizing the responsibility he will carry on his shoulders.

He taps his bride lightly with a switch while they circle a mat containing offerings three times.

An aunt leads the way with a lit palm frond.

A relative lights a fire for the couple to cook their first meal together.

What are those old coins used in offerings?
Chinese Kepeng

The groom 'buys' his bride with these ancient bronze coins which were used as currency in the 19th century. They are still used for weight measurements.

Entering their new life together, the couple breaks through a thread strung between two branches of a dapdap tree. Symbolizing their sexual union, the bride holds a small mattress woven from palm fronds while the groom pierces it with his ceremonial kris.

Why does the groom carry a dagger?

The Balinese Kris

Thought to contain spiritual energy, a family's kris is handed down through generations. It is kept in the family temple and purified every year.

Attendants burn incense and touch the couple's hands and feet with a mixture of egg, betel leaf and rice, asking the Gods to witness the union and to ensure fertility.

What's so special about the Dapdap tree?

The Dapdap tree

The Coral tree with its clusters of three leaves—representing Vishnu, Shiva and Brahma—is revered for its fast-growing properties and is often used in ceremonies.

❷ Other friends and family hold on to a long, white cloth, symbolically helping to carry the deceased.

❹ # Bade/Wadah
The remains of the deceased are transported to the cremation site in a tall tower representing heaven and earth.

❶ # Pura Dalem
The cremation takes place outside of the village in the cemetery grounds of the Temple of the Dead. Villagers carrying close family members of the deceased on a palanquin arrive first, followed by other processionists. They circle the cremation tent three times before placing the offerings inside.

Why so raucous? Shouldn't this be a sad event?

❸ The wooden sarcophagus in the shape of a bull is spun and tilted back and forth to confuse the spirit of the deceased and stop it from returning to the village and creating trouble.

Won't I be intruding if I attend the funeral of a perfect stranger?

Cremations are joyous events. Anyone dressed respectively in a sarung is welcomed to attend.

Bhoma is a symbol of the Son of Earth, and sits above the photo of the deceased on the funeral tower.

Who is the scary guy on the back of the tower?

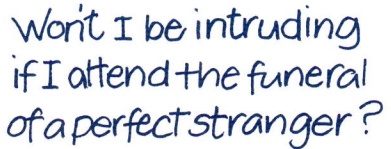

Pelebon
Cremation

❺ The sarcophagus is placed under a large awning. The body is carried down from the top of the tower—again in a rowdy manner.

Cremation in Bali is a ceremony for renewal and purification of the soul, deemed necessary so that it can return and inhabit the body of a new family member.

❻ A high priest prays and sprinkles holy water over the bull. Logs below the sarcophagus are lit. It is believed that the soul is lifted to heaven on a column of smoke. The ashes are raked and the charred bones are collected then dispersed over the sea.

Performances of dance, music and theater entertain the Gods and the spectators alike.

Isn't there going to be a puppet play tonight?

Wayang Kulit
Shadow puppet performances of Hindu epics take place after midnight and last several hours.

Odalan
Temple Anniversary Festivals

Everyone enjoys these religious celebrations that last for three days and involve preparations that take many weeks. An Odalan is held in each temple every 210 days and is a time when the Gods are welcomed back to their temples and entertained. Every family brings an offering and is blessed by a priest before enjoying the carnival-like atmosphere.

Colorful processions of women carrying tall offerings on their head arrive throughout the day. Groups from the village association will often dress alike in fine woven and brocaded fabrics, creating a beautiful scene.

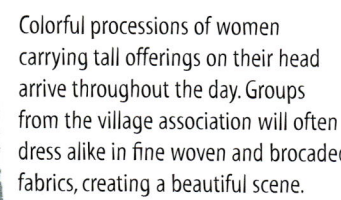

Families come in the cool of the evening and shop at the many toy and food stalls lining the entrance. Everyone dresses in their finest clothes, with the men in white and gold, and the women in bright colors.

Offerings are placed in an open pavilion to be blessed by a priest. Groups kneel down in the temple's central courtyard to pray.

What are those tall hats women wear on their heads?

Banten Tegeh
Truly works of art, these tall offerings with fruit, sweets, and sometimes meat are created at home and transported to the temple, often on a woman's head.

Is that a pile of trash?

Caru, a large mound of old offerings and refuse, is set aside in the temple for the demons to feed upon.

Muspa/Mabakti Praying

To whom do the Balinese pray?

Prayers are said to the Supreme God Sanghyang Widi and other deities.

Aren't there any pews to sit on?

Men sit cross-legged on the ground while women kneel with toes tucked under the feet.

Shoes are never worn while praying but the toes can rest on top of flip flops.

While praying, the Balinese people follow an elaborate ritual. Each person sits or kneels with a bowl of previously blessed flowers in front of them and a stick of incense stuck upright in the ground.

Hands in supplication should be raised to forehead height, thumbs pointed or touching the forehead with fingers upright.

❶ Remove your shoes. Sit down. Light the incense. Wash your hands with a few flower petals and discard.

❷ To begin praying, place hands over incense and immediately bring them up to the forehead. In the first prayer no flower is needed.

❸ For the second prayer place a white frangipani flower between the first and second fingers of both hands and bring them up to your forehead. Discard the flower or put it in your hair.

❹ For the third prayer a Kwangen offering is used. Repeat the process two more times, the last time without holding a flower. Place hands over the incense again.

what is that small bowl atop the offering?

Saab
A bowl used to hold flowers during prayers.

Dupa
Incense wafts the essence of offering to the Gods.

Kwangen
An offering of flowers and a Chinese coin

Pemangku
or a temple priest, anoints the faithful with holy water collected from a sacred spring.

❺ The priest passes by and annoints everyone with holy water—sprinkling each person three times.

❻ To receive the holy water, hold your right hand on the left. Sip the water and wipe your hands over your head.

❼ This step is repeated two more times. Wipe your hands on your face and head on the second time.

❽ Next, the priest offers a small dab of rice called a *bija*. Receive it in the right hand then transfer it to the left.

❾ With the right hand dab some on the forehead, then the throat and in the mouth.

❿ Any leftover bits are placed on the hair. The priest sprinkles holy water again.

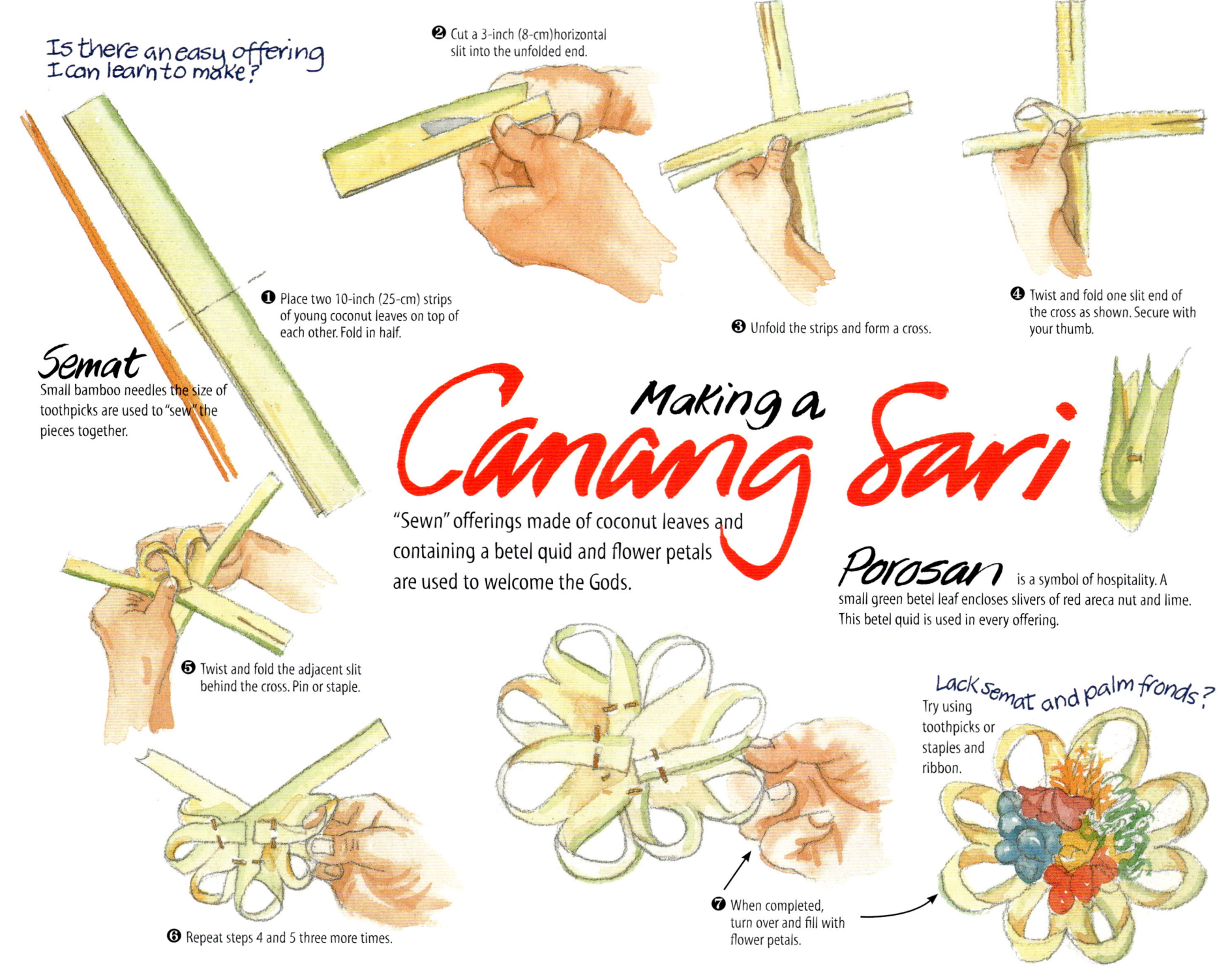

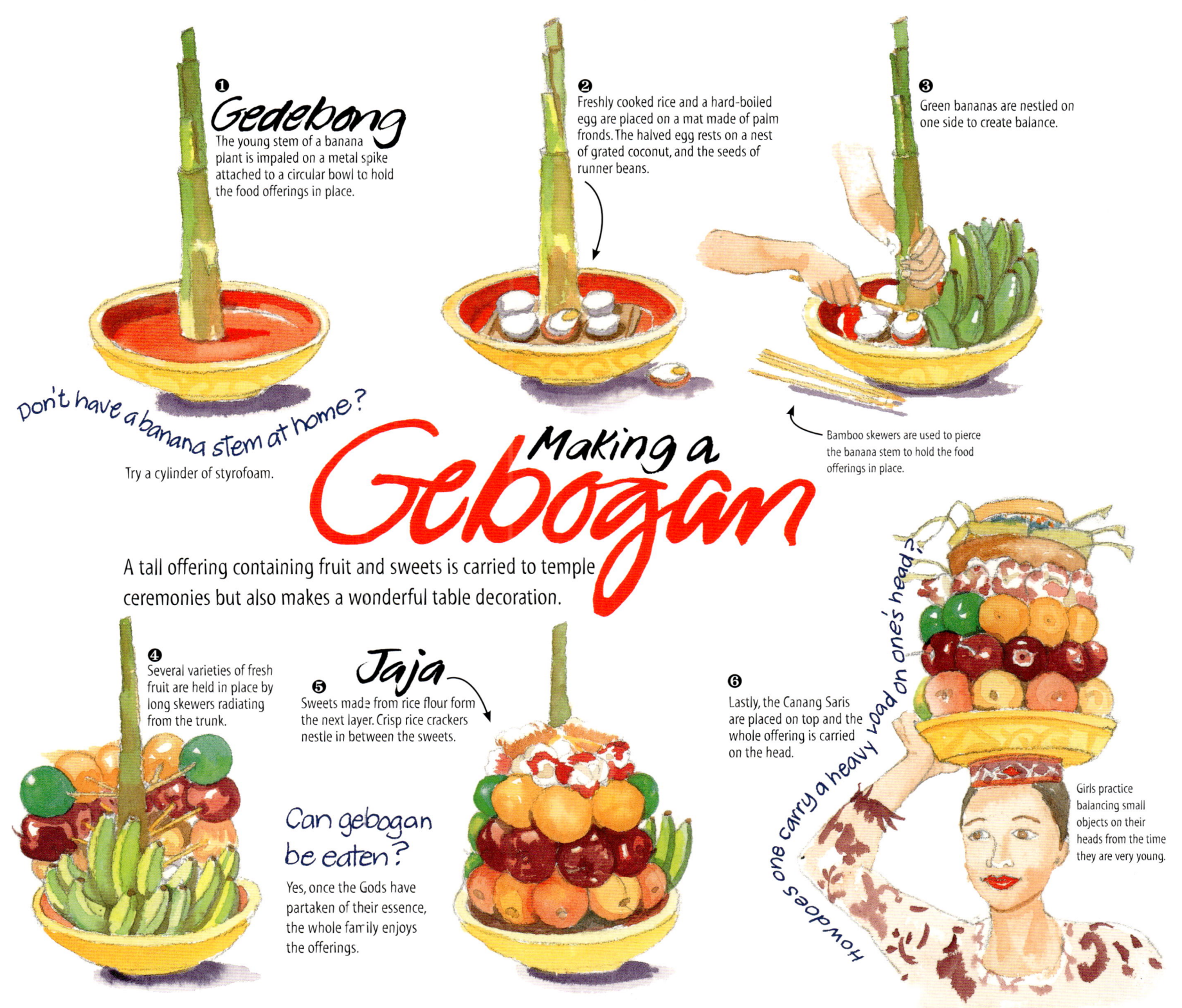

The Kamben
Traditional Clothing

Although the Balinese have adopted western garb for everyday wear, traditional clothing is always worn to ceremonies and temple festivals.

Do women wear a head scarf?
No, women usually wear their freshly washed hair neatly tied back in a bun.

How do I tie a sarung? And isn't it called a sarong?
Sarong is an Indonesian word but in Balinese, it is spelled *sarung*.

Udeng
Head cloth

It is believed that the udeng, the sarung and the sash keep the wearer's mind and body pure and ready to communicate with the Gods.

Women's Sarung/Kamben
Just follow the illustrations. Don't worry if the cloth doesn't wrap around you as many times as on a lithe Balinese. <u>Do</u> make sure it is secure.

Kebaya
Long-sleeved blouse

Selempot
Sash

Sarung/Kamben
Wrapped skirt

Saput
Covering for the men's sarung

Is a man's sarung tied differently?

Men's Sarung/Kamben

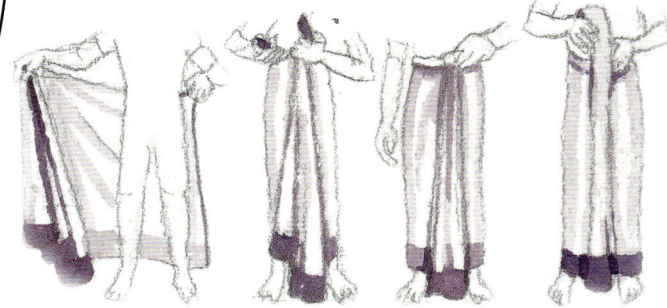

❶ Gather a drape with several folds in the right hand.
❷ Wrap the sarung around you so the drape is in the front.
❸ Roll down the top to form a waistband.
❹ Pull up the draped panel if necessary so the bottom is level.

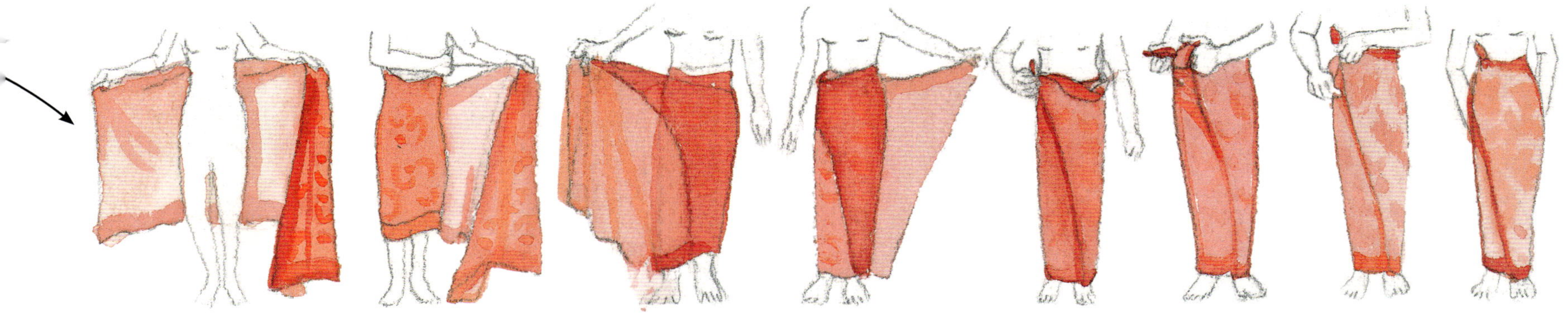

Tying an udeng

❶ Fold a large square into a triangle.

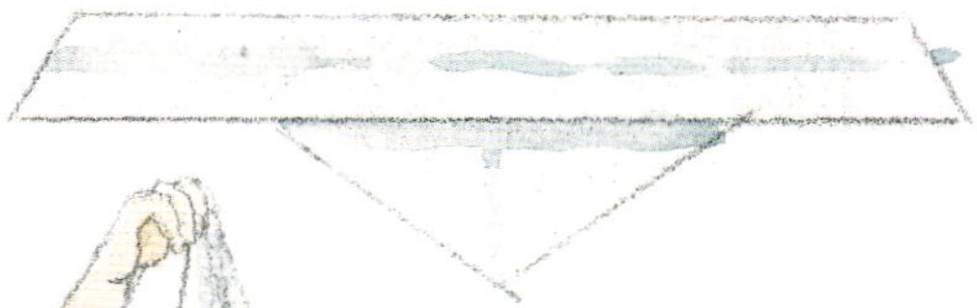

❷ Fold down the upper third.

❸ Fold the upper third in half to form a band.

❹ Center on head.

❺ Hold it loosely in the back, with one hand.

❻ Pull up on the crown with the other.

❼ Bring the two ends of the band to the front.

❽ Tie the ends in a small knot and tie them again.

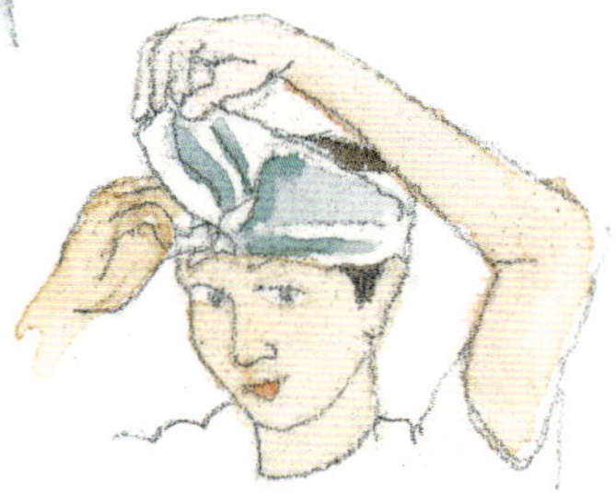

❾ Pull up on the crown and tuck the corner under the knots.

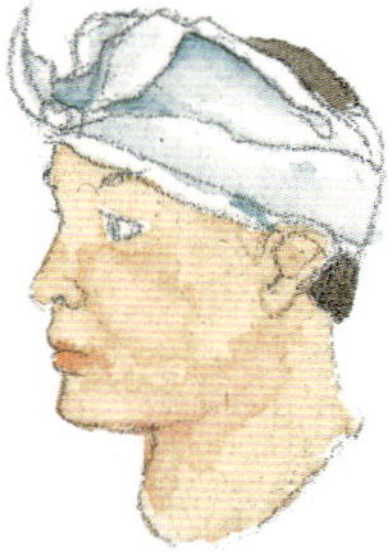

❿ **Voila!** The finished look. (Or you can always buy a ready-made udeng at the market.)

Men's saput

when is a saput worn?
A saput is added for religious events and ceremonies.

❶ Center the saput around your body.

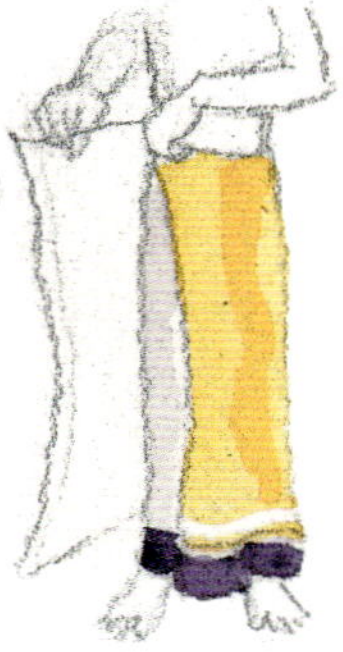

❷ Wrap the left side around you, then the right.

❸ Tighten it and roll down.

❹ Tie the sash on the left side.

❺ Hopefully the sash will hold it all together, but if not, use a belt under the saput.

❺ Tuck the upper portion under the rolled waist band.

At the beginning of the ceremony, the head of the household lights incense, recites mantras and offers prayers to the god of animals.

Offerings for the gods and ancestors are placed in each shrine and altar.

What is a tumpek?

Tumpek is a day set aside to honor the Gods associated with important disciplines such as art, drama, learning and prosperity. Other Tumpeks are held for valued objects like trees, books, computers, vehicles, musical instruments, puppets, and modern appliances.

The family cow and pigs are bathed, blessed and given a treat.

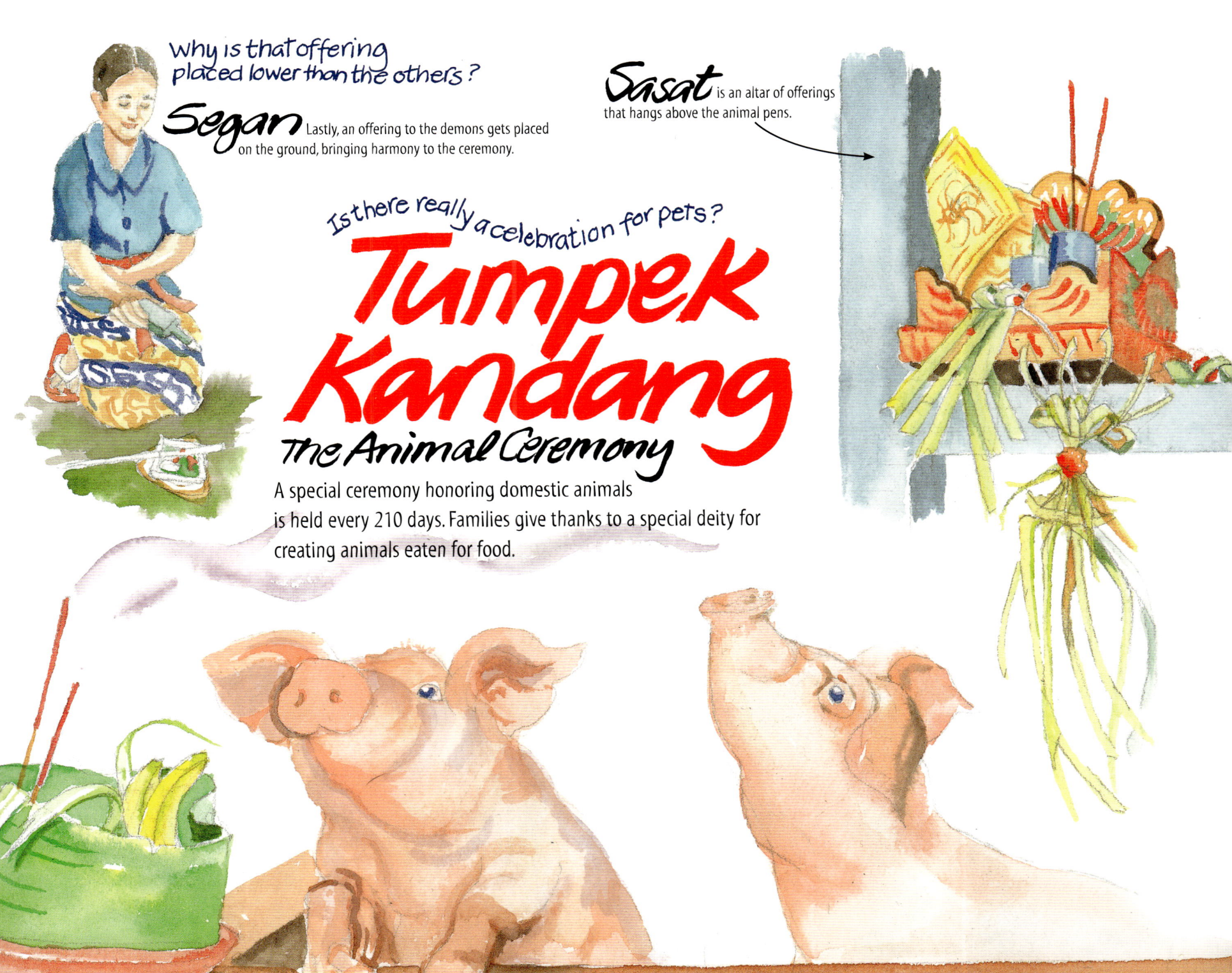

Babi Guling
Suckling pig with crispy skin

Look for these delicious, traditional meals when you are in Bali.

Tum Ayam
Steamed chicken with spice paste in banana leaves

Nasi Campur
Rice with chicken, peanuts and vegetables

Bebek
Delicious duck is served crispy or cooked in a banana leaf with spices.

Ikan Pepes
Grilled fish in a banana leaf

The Balinese prefer to eat with their fingers. Give it a try!

Excuse me? Where are my utensils?

Lawar
Bali's signature dish is a salad made with jackfruit, spices, veggies and pig parts.

Sate Lilit
Meals to go—meat or fish grilled on skewers

Buah
Fruits

Tropical fruit in Bali is certainly exotic. How can anything that looks so forbidding taste so good?

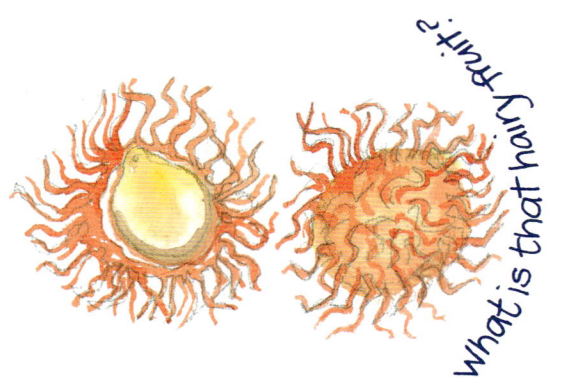

Rambutan — *what is that hairy fruit?*
Once you crack open the spiky exterior you'll find a delectable morsel similar to a lychee.

Sirsak — *Is that a fruit or a weapon?*
The juicy "sour sack" or soursop is made into juices and desserts.

Durian — *Yikes! what is that odor?*
The "king of fruit" has a custardy flavor and a pungent odor so strong it has been banned from hotels and airplanes. Lovers of this fruit say it tastes like heaven but stinks like hell. Definitely an acquired taste.

Nangka, or jackfruit, can grow up to 110 pounds. The orange flesh, sold in sections, has a strong flavor and smell. Don't store it uncovered in the refrigerator.

What is that large, lumpy thing hanging from trees?

Apples, bananas and citrus are used in towering offerings.

Srikaya
The custard apple has a sweet, soft flesh similar to the soursop.

Fresh fruit juices can be found at roadside stands.

Manggis
A mangosteen has a crumbly outer shell with delicious white flesh inside.

The number of petals on the outside bottom tells you how many segments there are inside.

Salak — *What is that thing with the lizard skin?*
The 'snakefruit' has a thin, scaly skin. When you peel it off, you find a small cluster of white segments with a taste similar to an apple.

Tiang Matur Suksama
Thank you very much!

My sincere thanks to I Wayan Legit, his wife Ni Wayan Suri; I Made Dwi Sutaryantha, his wife Nyoman Kawiwati; and Putu Tono for their patience and guidance in Balinese culture. Additional gratitude goes to all of the Balinese people who welcomed us into their homes and shared their celebrations with us.

This book would not have been possible without the help of Eric Oey and Genna Manaog of Periplus Editions; Lisa and George Presanis; and Marcy and John Ashoff.